Bayani Biographies

Andres Bonifacio

written by

John Ray Ramos

Michael Charleston "Xiao" Chua

Bayani Biographies: Andres Bonifacio

Published in 2019 by St. Matthew's Publishing Corporation
(through its imprint Kahel Press)

ISBN 978-971-625-422-8

Order individual copies from www.stmatthews.ph
Copies are also available at special rates in bulk orders. Contact the publisher through the details below.

St. Matthew's Publishing Corporation
First RVC Building, 92 Anonas Cor. K-6th Streets,
East Kamias, Quezon City
(02) 8426-5611 || inquiry@stmatthews.ph
www.stmatthews.ph

Foreword

Andres Bonifacio is honored as one of the nation's greatest heroes. He was the foremost founder and leader of the *Katipunan*, the secret society that in 1896 launched the revolution against Spanish rule in the Philippines.

Many well-known Filipinos, including Jose Rizal, also wanted independence from Spain, but believed it should be gained by peaceful means, and wished first to work for reforms – changes that would make Spanish rule less harsh and unjust, would improve the education system, and would bring economic progress. They said it was too soon to launch the revolution because the people were not yet ready.

They also warned that the revolution was doomed to fail, because the Katipunan did not have many guns. The vast majority of the Katipunan's fighters could carry only bolos and knives into battle, whilst the Spanish forces had modern rifles. Even some Katipunan leaders, including Emilio Aguinaldo, initially wanted to delay the revolution for this reason.

But in August 1896, when the Spaniards discovered the Katipunan, delay ceased to be an option. The choices facing the Katipuneros were limited, and hard. To abandon the cause of freedom?

To stay at home, waiting to be arrested or worse? To hide in the hills, perhaps for years? Most agreed it would be better to fight, even though they were ill-prepared and ill-equipped. They foresaw the battles ahead would be tough, and that many of them would be killed.

But their dying breath, wrote Bonifacio, would "be the breath that gives life to our nation.... Our side is in the right. Ours are noble deeds... The Spaniards are fighting for the wrong... [because they are] oppressing a nation that is not theirs."

Today, few would disagree. At that time, however, Bonifacio's sentiments were radical and trailblazing. They heralded an era of militant nationalism not just in the Philippines but across the region. In other Southeast Asian countries, as in the Spanish Philippines, resistance to foreign domination dated back centuries, but nowhere else in the 1890s was there any organization like the Katipunan. "Modern" nationalist organizations were not founded in French Indo-China, the Netherlands East Indies or British Malaya until the twentieth century.

The Katipunan's ideals were liberty ("*kalayaan*"), equality ("*lahat ng tao'y magkakapantay*"), and fraternity ("*lahat ay magkakapatid*"). Its leaders hoped the nation to be born would be guided by reason ("*katuiran*") and enlightenment ("*kaliwanagan*"). The Katipunan was also "modern" in other ways. It wanted to involve all Filipinos in the struggle for freedom—the poor as well as the rich, the unschooled as well as the learned, women as well as men. It was the first political organization in the country to appeal in Tagalog to the masses of ordinary people who did not know Spanish. Its leaders were elected by its members and activists, and when the revolution started even its military commanders were elected by their troops. The Katipunan pioneered democratic principles and practices, in other words, long before the nation itself was to become a democracy.

Telling the remarkable story of Bonifacio and the Katipunan is a difficult, challenging task for historians. On countless details, the sources are few and conflicting, and leave so many secrets untold.

In the past few years, however, documents have come to light that fill some of the gaps in our knowledge and correct some of our past misunderstandings. This excellent book by John Ray Ramos and Michael Charleston "Xiao" Chua is one of the first to take account of the latest discoveries about Bonifacio and the Katipunan. Though aimed mainly at younger readers, it therefore deserves to be read too by college students, who will find that it augments and updates earlier works.

The authors are also to be commended for recounting Bonifacio's life against the background of his times, for setting his heroic patriotism in its economic, social and political context. For some, the rapid changes seen in the late nineteenth century Philippines brought a new prosperity. But in the hearts of Bonifacio and his fellow Katipuneros they aroused a burning sense of justice, and a fierce desire to be free.

Jim Richardson
London
July 2019

Introduction

This is the story of Andres Bonifacio, someone who dreamt of a better future for his countrymen. For more than three hundred years, Filipinos were subjected to unfair colonial rule. They were not treated as equals in their very country. Despite the many odds Andres faced, he took on the dangerous task to start the fight for freedom and for the birth of the Filipino nation.

The sources about Andres vary in detail as well as in perspective, many of which conflict with one another as many people have different opinions about him. Aside from this, the story of Andres's life is full of misconceptions. He had the reputation of being uneducated, badly tempered, and violent. This narrative includes the Katipunan which was mistaken to be composed only of poor, uneducated people who quickly charged into battle.

But historians, through time, have corrected many such misconceptions and myths surrounding Andres's life. This biography looks at Andres as a brother, a best friend, an artist, a thinker, an entrepreneur, an activist, a leader and a revolutionary who inspired the Filipino people to fight for liberty.

TABLE OF CONTENTS

The Boy from Manila

It was the 30th day of November in 1863 when a newborn baby was heard crying in a house in the province of Manila. He was the first child of the six children that Santiago and Catalina would have.

Andres Bonifacio was born on the feast day of San Andres Apostol or St. Andrew the Apostle, one of the patron saints of Manila. Andres got his name from the patron saint whose feast day was on his day of birth as was the custom in the Philippines during the rule of the Spaniards.

Spanish Colonial Period

Spain colonized the Philippines in the 16th century bringing the *Indios* or native Filipinos under the rule of the Spanish King. The colonized Filipinos were converted into Christianity by Spanish Friars and in this process, the old history, culture, and way of life of Filipinos changed.

They were also subjected to Spanish laws but were not considered equals to Spaniards.

Supported by the Spanish friars who were highly influential in the towns and provinces, the Spanish Governor General ruled the archipelago in behalf of the King. The community leaders of the Filipinos, the *gobernadorcillos* (town mayors) and heads of barangays, are to follow the orders of the Spanish friars and officials.

Andres's mother, Catalina de Castro, was from Zambales. She worked in a tobacco factory. She worked so well that she became a *cabecilla* or table manager and eventually a *maestra* or supervisor of the women's section of the factory. Since her father was a Spaniard, she was a *mestiza* or one of mixed Spanish heritage.

Meanwhile, his father, Santiago Bonifacio, who was from Taguig used to work as a boatman ferrying people across Laguna de Bai to Taytay. There, the strong and hardworking Santiago met Catalina and fell in love with each other. He moved to Tondo where he worked as a *cargador* or porter carrying goods from the docks to shops around Binondo and where he also did some tailoring work for extra income.

The couple married in Tondo on January 24, 1863. They built a nipa house in a plot of land in a community called Tutuban.

Their first son Andres was followed by Ciriaco, Procopio, Espiridiona, Troadio, and Maxima. The siblings fondly called their eldest brother "Manong Andres." They were a big family living in a small house.

The Bonifacio family lived a simple life. On Sundays and holidays, the whole family would attend mass at the Tondo Church. They were a religious family. Andres's parents were religious and they taught their children prayers and catechism.

Years of hard work as a porter took a toll on their father's health that he changed his occupation to tailoring and doing crafts. He made wooden chairs, *abanikos* or folding hand fans, and *bastones* or walking canes which were sold to Spaniards and richer Filipinos. Later on, Santiago's brother, Hermogenes Bonifacio joined them in the household and helped in making the crafts they sold.

Andres and his siblings were taught from a young age to value hard work and honest living. Their father Santiago taught them how to make *abanikos* to sell. Andres was taught to make walking canes out of wood and rattan which he would teach to his younger brothers. Selling their crafts added to the earnings of the family. The wooden crafts like the canes they hand-carved and polished were of good quality and sold very well.

Catalina was Andres's first teacher. She taught him how to read and write. He later studied in a school near their house owned by Don Guillermo Osmeña from Cebu. He then also studied in a school along Calle Ilaya in Tondo headed by a Don Epifanio del Castillo. Andres was able to finish his studies in what was the equivalent of elementary school until he reached the third year of secondary education. Andres had to stop schooling to help in their family business. Despite this, Andres did not stop studying on his own.

Andres made time to study. He studied hard to improve his skills in speaking the Spanish language. After working to make fans and canes, he would spend his time reading. He believed that learning Spanish could give him better opportunities at work.
Andres and his younger siblings lived a busy but content life with the ample earnings of their parents and their home business. There were lots of opportunities to earn money as their community around Manila in the last decades of the 19th century was starting to experience growth due to the businesses setting up shop around the area.

Booming Manila

For more than two centuries since it was established as a Spanish colony, the Philippines was not open to trade with other European countries. This changed in the early 1800s when Spain's Galleon Trade with Mexico, another Spanish colony, ended because of the Mexican war for independence. This led to Spain losing Mexico which established an independent government in 1821.

The Galleon Trade was the main economic activity of the Spaniards in the Philippines for more than two centuries where only they profited from the luxury goods like silk and porcelain from China being shipped and sold for silver in Mexico. The Spanish Colonial Government in the Philippines then started economic reforms in the country and by 1834, allowed foreign companies to do business in the Philippines.

During the time of Andres, the City of Manila was limited only to the area inside the walls of Intramuros, the old city where the seat of power of the Spanish colonial government and major friar orders were located. Areas around it, primarily the districts of Quiapo, Santa Cruz, Binondo, and San Nicolas, parts of the province of Manila, were areas where businesses had taken root. Trading companies from European countries had established their offices and warehouses in the said districts. Businesses owned by enterprising Filipinos had set up shop as well.

This economic growth was further enhanced by Manila's location. The area near Manila was a bustling port area and the banks of the Pasig River had

wharves for loading and unloading goods for trade. Pasig River and the *esteros* or waterways of Binondo provided routes for goods. By 1892, the *ferrocaril* or the railroad from Manila to Dagupan in Pangasinan opened. The railyard and the main station were built where the Bonifacio family's nipa house once stood.

With all the business activities in the districts around Manila, there were opportunities for Filipinos to earn and provide for the needs of their families.

The Bonifacio family fell into hard times in 1883 when their father was stricken with tuberculosis and became bedridden. Andres had to work more to help support the family.

In 1885, their household was blessed with the birth of their youngest member, Maxima. Unfortunately, it was at the cost of their mother's life. Catalina died at childbirth and after 10 months, their father Santiago also died. This left Andres and his younger siblings as orphans. The 22-year-old Andres became one of the family's breadwinners. He became responsible for taking care of his younger siblings.

THE YOUNG PROFESSIONAL

Andres worked hard and balanced his time between his daytime job, taking care of his siblings, and other entrepreneurial activities. Their aunt, the wife of their uncle Hermogenes, helped their family as well.

One day, members of the *guardia civil* came to their house for their uncle Hermogenes. He was beaten badly with their rifles and was taken away. He was arrested for avoiding mandatory labor and military service under the Spanish Rule. He was sent to exile to Puerto Princesa in Palawan. At first, the Bonifacio family did not know where he was exiled to.

Guardia Civil

The Guardia Civil was an organization of the Spanish Colonial government established in 1868. It was equivalent to a police force. The organization was headed by Spanish officers and were manned by Filipinos in the ranks. They were tasked with keeping the community safe and arresting those who committed crimes.

Unfortunately, the guardia civil had a bad reputation because of their abusive behavior. They would beat suspected criminals and even shoot them without trial at court. They were constantly on the lookout for any activities or groups suspected of being against the colonial government.

Their aunt eventually learned about where Hermogenes was exiled to and she decided to follow him there. Andres and his siblings were all that remained in the household.

Andres had to take different jobs around the busy districts of Manila to support his siblings. He was a professional calligrapher. He did formal lettering for signages and letters used in business by other people. This was one of his means to earn additional money for his family. By practicing a lot, he developed his own calligraphy style in writing.

Andres also established and became active in a local theater troupe called *Teatro Porvenir* in nearby Quiapo district. Andres was into singing and acting. He and his friends Macario Sakay and the playwright Aurelio Tolentino were active members of this theater troupe performing *comedias* or *moro-moro* plays. Many of these plays were satirical about events and personalities in Philippine colonial society. Andres's favorite role, among many roles, was that of the legendary Bernardo Carpio.

The Legend of Bernardo Carpio

When the Spaniards colonized the Philippines, they erased the old history and literature of Filipinos. Filipinos adjusted and created new epics allowed and influenced by the Spaniards. The *awit* or songs were stories that were dramatized and sung in public with stories from European history and legends talking about kings and heroes in wars. An example would be *Florante at Laura* by Francisco Balagtas.

Another awit was that of Spanish hero Bernardo Carpio who defeated the Moors and French in war. The epic in Tagalog was *Historia Famosa de Bernardo Carpio* published and popularized in the 19th century. Also popular was the awit about the life of Christ called *Pasiong Mahal* (Holy Passion).

Both *Florante at Laura* and *Bernardo Carpio*, despite having European topics, were written by Filipino writers in a way that the characters reflected the plight of Filipinos also suffering injustice under colonial rule.

The literary epics mixed with the beliefs of the people. The Tagalogs eventually believed in folklore that Bernardo Carpio was their legendary king trapped between the mountains of San Mateo in the Province of Morong (now called the Province of Rizal). They believed that earthquakes were signs that Carpio was struggling to break free and that the day would come when Carpio would set himself free and end the harsh rule of the Spaniards. The literature of the people like that of Bernardo Carpio read and loved by Andres reflected the Filipinos' true yearning for freedom.

Andres always carried a book with him. During his lunch break or downtime, he was always seen with his nose buried in the book he was reading. He stayed up late at night and sometimes did not sleep just so that he could read.

Andres the Booklover

Andres had a personal library at home and in his office. He read both history books and novels written in the Spanish language as well as works in Tagalog. Here were some of the books, or versions thereof, in his library:

- *The Count of Monte Cristo* by Alexander Dumas
- *The Wandering Jew* by Eugene Sue
- *The Ruins of Palmyra: Meditations on the Revolution of the Empire* by C.F. Volney
- *Les Miserables* by Victor Hugo
- *The French Revolution*
- B*iographic History of the Presidents of the United States*

One of his favorites, *The Wandering Jew*, was a legend of a Jew who mocked Jesus Christ at the cross and was cursed to walk the earth until the second Coming of Christ. Andres also had books about law and justice, international rights, the civil code, and the penal code of their time.

One of his favorites was *Florante at Laura* by Francisco Balagtas which he performed in theater and knew by heart. Because he grew up in a religious family, he also knew the *Pasiong Mahal* or the Holy Passion, a Tagalog epic about the life of Christ published in 1704.

Andres also had books that were banned in the Philippines by Spanish colonial authorities. These included the writings of Filipino activists like the novels *Noli me Tangere* and *El Filibusterismo* by Jose Rizal and copies of *La Solidaridad*, the newspaper of Filipino activists in Europe. Anyone caught with these materials were arrested. Andres safely stashed them in his office in C. Fressel & Co.

Andres met and fell in love with Monica, a neighbor from the nearby barrio Palomar in Tondo. But tragedy struck as Monica was afflicted with and died from leprosy.

In 1886, the Bonifacio house was bought by J.M. Fleming, a British company supplying construction materials for the train station and railyard of the planned *ferrocarril* or railroad. The Bonifacio family transferred to Tondo near the church. It was at this time as well that Andres applied for a job in the same company. Because of his good handwriting and industriousness, he was hired as a clerk. He wrote letters which the company sent out to its clients. He also became a messenger to deliver notes to the company's clients and employees. Because of his hard work and trustworthiness, he was promoted as an agent to sell tar, rattan, *sahing* (pili resin) and other things that the company sold.

As a professional, Andres dressed smartly. He was said to have always worn an open coat and a black tie over his camisa and white trousers. He also wore a black hat and always carried an umbrella.

In 1891, Andres transferred and was hired as a *bodeguero* for C. Fressel & Co., a German trading firm, for a higher wage. The *bodeguero* handled the inventory of the products that were sold and stored in the warehouse. This job required one to be attentive to details as well as to be honest and trustworthy.

In 1892, Andres and the rest of the family moved to a new home in an apartment along Calle Sagunto (now Santo Cristo Street). At the same apartment, Andres accommodated his friends Ladislao Diwa, Teodoro Plata and Aurelio Tolentino. They lived together under the same roof and shared with each other the warmth of home and ideas for a better future, not just for their families, but for the whole country.

Alias "MAYPAGASA"

Andres and his friends were busy with their personal lives and careers yet they were aware of the issues that affected their fellow countrymen. Just as what happened to his uncle Hermogenes, many Filipinos suffered injustices and hardships in the hands of Spanish friars and officials. Andres and his friends talked about these problems and pondered on what to do to help their motherland. They decided to do something and began planning for the creation of an organization that would help bring good change to the country.

Injustices Under Spanish Rule

Life in the Philippines as a Spanish Colony was oftentimes not favorable to Filipinos. Filipinos were unfairly treated in many ways.

Before the time of Andres, the old system of the encomienda placed large areas of the archipelago under the control of ***encomenderos*** who were assigned to rule over the land and its people. The *encomenderos* taxed and worked native Filipinos too much and did little to improve their welfare.

Polos y servicios was a program that required all *indio* males 16-60 years old to give 40 days of work to government for public works. Many were taken to faraway places, given extended days for labor or did not return at all. Workers were underpaid and underfed. Should one wish to avoid enlistment into the program, the native had to pay a fee called the *falla*. Anybody who avoided the compulsory work or the payment of the *falla* was jailed. The polo was already removed by the time Andres was born.

The ***bandala*** required farmers to produce

and sell their crops to the government. Yet, the government purchased these products at very low prices or did not pay for them at all.

Also, ***haciendas*** were vast tracks of land owned by a single person, family or corporation. The Spanish friars owned many of the haciendas which they leased to enterprising farmers. The friars charged the native Filipino farmers exorbitant fees. *Hacenderos* also expanded their land by grabbing or titling the untitled lands adjacent to their hacienda despite the land being tilled by a Filipino family for generations.

Filipinos also faced unfair treatment in courts. Friars could order the arrest of individuals on trivial charges. Being arrested often meant long periods in jail along with expensive and slow trial procedures. Filipinos hardly expected to be served justice if they were accused by Spaniards or Spanish friars.

By the 19th century, Filipinos were required to pay their community tax and were issued a ***cedula*** which also serves as their identification card. While patrolling the streets, members of the guardia civil regularly checked cedulas. Failure to show a cedula could lead to one being beaten and jailed.

Despite the economic opportunities at the time, Filipinos faced a bleak situation where they were treated unfairly in their own country.

Andres knew about the Filipinos involved in the Propaganda Movement. They had members in Spain and other parts of Europe who pushed for reforms in the Philippines. They wanted the Philippines to be a Spanish province, its inhabitants to be given equal rights, and to have improved education and justice systems. The movement also wanted Filipino priests to be the ones who will lead parishes instead of Spanish friars. Its members included Jose Rizal, Marcelo H. del Pilar, Mariano Ponce, and brothers Juan and Antonio Luna. They aspired for the Philippines to eventually and peacefully separate from Spain.

Despite the efforts of the propagandists, the situation in the Philippines did not improve. Even if there were lots of opportunities for businesses, the prices of goods produced in the Philippines like sugar were not stable. This led to many Filipino farmers to be driven away from their homes because they were unable to pay the land they leased from the Spanish friars.

In January of 1892, Ladislao Diwa, a friend of Andres, drafted a document called "*Casaysayan*; *Pinagcasundoan*, *Manga daquilang cautosan*" or "Narrative; Covenant; and Principal Orders." This was a plan for an organization that would lead and fight for freedom from the Spaniards.

In the document, it was stated that separation from Spain was necessary to bring about change in the Philippines. The document was a proclamation of independence stating that the Philippine Islands were separate from Spain and that the Supreme Katipunan was the only authority and government that they recognized.

Andres and his friends heard of a new organization, La Liga Filipina, being organized by the famous propagandist, Jose Rizal, who had just returned from Hong Kong in June of 1892.

Jose Rizal and the Katipunan

Rizal was an important figure to the Katipunan. He wrote about the injustices experienced by his countrymen at the hands of friars and fellow Filipinos under the abusive colonial system. Jose described these systemic problems as a social cancer that afflicted Philippine society which he exposed in his controversial novel *Noli me Tangere*. Jose became a figure known to many Filipinos as someone who stood up against injustices. He called out the abuses of friar landlords to farmer tenants in the haciendas as well as the unfair treatment of Filipinos in their native land.

Even before the revolution, the *katipuneros* held Jose in high regard as an inspirational figure who stood up against colonial injustices. Without his knowledge, Jose was made honorary president of the Katipunan.

His name was also used as a password for officers and in every secret meeting his portrait was displayed. Jose's brother Paciano and two sisters, Josefa and Trinidad, became members of the Katipunan.

Upon his return, Jose met with people asking them to take part in the new organization he was establishing, the *La Liga Filipina*. The organization intended to bring change to the situation of their society through peaceful and legal means. Members would help one another in their need and against injustice, as well as encourage education, agriculture and business among themselves and other Filipinos.

On the evening of July 3, 1892, Andres attended the founding of La Liga Filipina in Binondo to take part in the advocacy. The house where the meeting was held was jam-packed with people who wanted to take part in the advocacy. This was the only time that Andres saw Jose in person, someone whose writings he read and whom he admired for his convictions.

Andres was optimistic that La Liga Filipina would flourish and bring change in the homeland. But three days later, Rizal was arrested. The Spanish colonial government declared that Rizal was an enemy of the state and of Catholicism. He was sent to exile in Dapitan and so La Liga Filipina lost its leader and eventually dissolved.

On the evening of July 7, 1892, Andres with his friends Deodato Arellano, Ladislao Diwa, Teodoro Plata, Valentin Diaz, Jose Dizon, and Briccio Pantas met in an apartment near the corner of Azcarraga Street (now C.M. Recto) and Salinas Street (now Elcano). The meeting formally established the secret organization they had been planning since January, the *Kataas-taasang Kagalanggalang na Katipunan ng mga Anak ng Bayan*

or the "The Highest, Most Venerable Association of the Sons and Daughters of the People" was born.

Andres served as the Secretary of the secret organization, and as every member of the organization used a code name, Andres took the name "Maypagasa" meaning "there is hope."

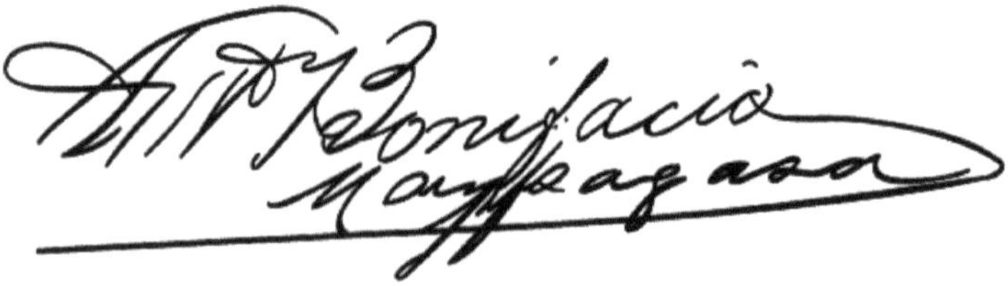

Life Inside the Katipunan

In October of 1892, the first Supreme Council of the Katipunan was created with Deodato Arellano as Supreme President. Andres remained as secretary.

Unfortunately, Arellano was not active in the budding organization. Andres moved to have him replaced on the grounds of not attending meetings and not attending to important matters. Roman Basa, a government clerk, became the new Supreme President.

In April of 1893, the dissolved La Liga Filipina was reestablished with Domingo Franco as president, Deodato Arellano as secretary-treasurer, and eventually with Apolinario Mabini as secretary. Andres rejoined the organization and took the alias "Sandakan," the name of a place in Sabah where Rizal planned to establish a Filipino colony. Andres headed the La Liga Filipina chapter "Mayon" in Trozo district.

As the Katipunan was starting and the La Liga Filipina was reorganizing, Andres was one of the most active organizers for both organizations he was in. He recruited members, started meetings, headed discussions in his chapter, and assisted other chapters. He performed his duties in both organizations. Most of the people he recruited in La Liga Filipina were from the masses, workers and professionals, who also eventually joined the Katipunan.

But soon differences among La Liga Filipina members became apparent. The La Liga Filipina suspended the Mayon Council that Andres headed for being too radical in its discussions and objectives. Andres disregarded this and continued to organize. It was found that an increasing number of members, many of whom were recruited by Andres, did not believe anymore in the peaceful means of change the organization aimed for. Also, the rich members looked down on its non-educated and not well-off members. With irreconcilable differences, the La Liga Filipina finally got disbanded in October 1893. Those with the same beliefs were already part of or would later on join the Katipunan.

It was also in 1893 when Andres courted Gregoria de Jesus, or Oriang. They met through Teodoro Plata, Andres's friend and fellow Katipunan founder who was also Oriang's cousin.

Andres and Oriang were married in March 1894 at the Parish Church of Binondo. Soon after, the two were also married in a secret ceremony officiated by the Katipunan. Oriang knew about the Katipunan and willingly joined her husband in the Filipinos' struggle for freedom. Oriang chose "Lakanbini" as her code name in the Katipunan.

Andres's Only Photograph

Andres Bonifacio had only one surviving photograph. Despite the popular imagery of Andres wearing a camisa, Andres in his only picture was wearing an *Americana*, or a suit. Andres typically wore a suit to work which was common to working professionals during his time.

This photo ended up in the hands of colonial authorities and was used as the basis of a sketch of Andres which was circulated as a wanted poster when the revolution broke out. This photo was published in a February 1897 issue of the newspaper *La Ilustración Española y America* wherein Andres was mentioned as the "President of the Tagalog Republic."

Andres and Oriang were both active leaders of the Katipunan. Oriang became a leader of the Women's Chapter of the movement and was responsible for the safekeeping of documents and seals of the Katipunan.

Andres found out that Teodoro Plata was secretly courting his younger sister, Espiridiona. As an overly protective brother, this incident made him very angry at his friend and colleague. He is said to have chased off Teodoro with a bolo. Eventually, after some time and seeing his friend's good intention and true love, Andres gave his permission for the two to be married.

Andres's brothers Procopio and Ciriaco also joined the Katipunan. In the movement, he also found another brother in the person of Emilio Jacinto, a young law student of the Universidad de Santo Tomas.

Emilio Jacinto

Andres and Emilio Jacinto had known each other since they were young. Both their mothers worked at the same tobacco factory. Josefa Dizon, Jacinto's mother, was a midwife and was the one who assisted Catalina in giving birth to Espiridiona on December 14, 1875.

Emilio Jacinto was born the next day, December 15. Catalina was of poor health and could not nurse the infant Espiridiona with breastmilk. It was Jacinto's mother who nursed the baby until she could eat soft foods. Since their mothers were close friends, the young Jacinto grew up knowing Andres as a big brother.

Jacinto's father died when he was young. His uncle Jose Dizon provided for his education enabling him to study in *Colegio de San Juan de Letran* and *Universidad de Santo Tomas*.

In 1894, Jacinto joined the Katipunan out of his own conviction and he took the alias "Pingkian" which meant the act of crossing swords. Emilio decided not to continue his studies to become active with the Katipunan. Together, Andres and Emilio Jacinto became the prominent writers of the Katipunan. He edited the *Kalayaan* and wrote with the pen name "Dimasilaw" or one who could not be blinded.

Emilio Jacinto eventually became the Supreme Secretary of the Katipunan.

Andres coached Emilio in writing Tagalog as the latter was not so proficient in the language. Emilio eventually became well-versed in writing in the language. One such document that displayed his skill in the language was the primer used in welcoming new members, the *Kartilya*. It stated that the foremost rule in the Katipunan was "true love of the native land and to have genuine compassion for one another."

KATIPUNAN

NANG MANGA

A. N. B.

SA MAY NASANG MAKISANIB
SA KATIPUNANG ITO

Sa pagkakailangan, na ang lahat na nagiibig pumasuk sa katipunang itó, ay magkaroon ng lubós na pananalig at kaisipán sa mga layong tinutungo at mga kaaralang pinaiiral, minarapat na ipakilala sa kanilá ang mga bagay na itó, at ng bukas makalawa'y huag siláng magsisi at tuparing maluag sa kalooban ang kaniláng mga tutungkulin.

Ang kabagayáng pinaguusig ng katipunang itó ay lubós na dakilà at mahalagá; papagisahin ang loob at kaisipan ng lahat ng tagalog (*) sa pamagitan ng isáng mahigpit na panunumpâ, upang sa pagkakaisáng itó'y magkalakás na iwasak ang masinsíng tabing na nakabubulag sa kaisipan at matuklasán ang tunay na landás ng Katuiran at Kaliwanagan.

(*) Sa salitang *tagalog* katutura'y ang lahat nang tumubo sa Sangkapuluang itó; sa makatuid, *bisaya* man, *iloko* man, *kapampangan* man, etc., ay *tagalog* din.

The objective of the Katipunan, according to the *Kartilya*, was to unite the hearts and minds of every Filipino. And with such unity, gain strength and destroy the veil that blinded everyone from seeing reason and discovering the path towards true enlightenment and freedom.

Andres's Decalogue

Andres and Emilio Jacinto each wrote a list of commandments pertaining to a moral code for the members of the Katipunan. Andres compared their works, and upon seeing that Emilio's work was far more superior than his, he opted to have Emilio's version used in the organization's primer.

Here is Andres's version:

10 Commandments to the Sons of the Nation

1. Love God with all your heart.
2. Remember always that true love to God also means to love the native land, which is also love of one another.
3. Plant in your heart that the real importance of honor and wellbeing is to offer your life for the salvation of the nation.
4. All of your good intentions will be fulfilled if you have patience, perseverance, righteousness and hope in your habits and endeavors.

5. Treasure the way you treasure your own honor the decisions and goals of the K.K.K..

6. It is the duty of everyone to save those on the verge of great danger to stay true to their duty even at the expense of one's life and possessions.

7. How we treat ourselves and how we take on our responsibilities will serve as an example to others.

8. Share what you can to those who are poor and in need.
9. The diligence you show in earning a

living is a genuine expression of love for yourself, for your partner, for your children, for your brothers, and for your countrymen.

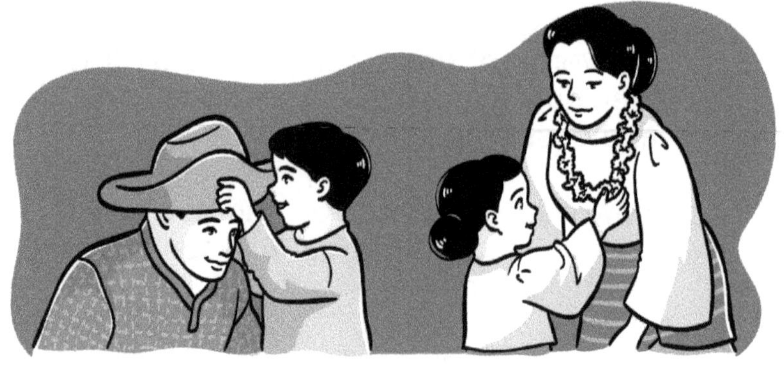

10. Punish scoundrels and traitors and praise good deeds. Believe that the ends of the K.K.K. are given by God; for the will of the motherland is also the will of God.

Despite not being used, this and other writings of Andres reflect his ideals on freedom. For him, true freedom meant everyone having *ginhawa* or well-being and living with *dangal* or dignity. This also meant actions motivated by *kapatiran* or brotherhood and *mabuting kalooban* or goodwill meaning having genuine concern for one another. This was the path which Andres and the Katipunan had laid out.

Leading the Katipunan

In late December of 1894, Andres was elected as *Kataas-taasang Pangulo* or Supreme President of the Katipunan. He became responsible for the overall leadership of the Katipunan and all its chapters.

Andres looked for locations where the katipuneros could establish their base at the start of the revolution. They went to the mountains of Morong and Bulacan looking for areas where Spanish forces would find a hard time attacking, where katipuneros could retreat, organize and launch attacks. Andres was preparing his *reales* or strongholds.

On one such occasion, a Good Friday, Andres and fellow katipuneros went to the mythical mountain of Bernardo Carpio believed to be in Mt. Tapusi in Montalban, Morong. In a symbolic gesture, they wrote on the walls of the Pamintinan cave, "*Mabuhay ang Kalayaan*!" (Long live freedom!) as a reaffirmation of their readiness to sacrifice their lives for the freedom of the nation.

In December 1895, Oriang gave birth to a baby boy. They named the baby Andres as well. Andres, Jr. was baptized on Christmas eve with Dr. Pio Valenzuela as godfather.

For three years, the Katipunan had only 300 members. Then, it was suggested that to propagate the goals of the Katipunan and recruit more members, the organization must publish a newspaper. Pio Valenzuela asked to be the one to carry out the publication. Andres agreed and entrusted him with the task. Emilio Jacinto then became its editor.

Kalayaan

The *Kalayaan* or "Freedom" was the name chosen by Pio Valenzuela for the newspaper of the Katipunan. Pio Valenzuela headed the publication team. The team was composed of Ulpiano Fernandez who was a printer for the newspaper El Comercio, Faustino Duque who was a student of Letran, and Emilio Jacinto. Printing started in January 16, 1896 in Valenzuela's home in Lavezares Street in San Nicolas. They worked at night to avoid being discovered. The first edition was limited to 8 pages because of scarcity of materials and slow printing. However, they were able to finish printing 2,000 copies by March.

To mislead authorities if a copy was captured, they printed Yokohama, Japan as the place of its publication and Marcelo H. del Pilar as editor who was in Spain but gravely sick.

The first and only edition of *Kalayaan* came out in March 1896. It had the writings of Andres, Emilio Jacinto and Pio Valenzuela. Andres's poems, Emilio Jacintos's treatise, and Pio Valenzuela's stories stated the harsh conditions under Spanish colonial and friar rule. It also promoted the ideals of the Katipunan of seeking true freedom through love of one another and working towards the good and well-being of the motherland.

Copies of the *Kalayaan* were distributed by Katipunan members in secret. Many read the *Kalayaan* and were inspired to join the Katipunan. With this, their numbers swelled from about 300 to 30,000.

Andres the Writer

Andres wrote his beliefs in the language understood by his countrymen. Here are some of the most important and enduring writings of Andres:

Pag-ibig sa Tinubuang Bayan
(Love of the Native Country)

In 1896, Andres wrote and published this poem in the Katipunan's newspaper, *Kalayaan*.

The poem described that the Motherland, the source of life of all Filipinos, was clenched in the claws of an evil tyrant. It called on Filipinos, the children of the Motherland, to defend her because helping the motherland would ultimately lead to the freedom and betterment of all.

Ang Dapat Mabatid ng mga Tagalog
(What Every Tagalog Should Know)

This essay told of the history of the Tagalogs who performed *sandugo* with the Spaniards. The ancient ritual of sandugo or blood compact was a means to seal the friendship of two peoples who performed the ritual. This symbolized brotherhood, respect and equality between them. In the essay, the Spaniards were described to have treated the Tagalogs as their slaves. Andres urged his Filipino readers to break away from this broken agreement with the Spaniards and to create a new blood compact with fellow Filipinos and to fight for their freedom and that of the Motherland.

Katapusang Hibik ng Pilipinas
(The Final Plea of the Philippines)

This poem, believed to be Andres's, served as a response to two other popular poems "*Hibik ng Pilipinas sa Inang Espanya*" (The Plea of the Philippines to Mother Spain) by Hermenegildo Flores, and "*Sagot ng Espanya sa Hibik ng Pilipinas*" written by propagandist Marcelo H. del Pilar. The former is a plea of the Philippines under harsh conditions and the latter is a satirical response of Spain to the prior plea. Andres's poem said that after 300 years of Spanish rule, Filipinos endured only suffering and that Spain was no longer the mother of Filipinos.

Andres also inaugurated new chapters of the Katipunan. He went around Bulacan, Cavite, and Morong where new chapters were opened, with new members learning about the movement through the local chapters and a publication.

Life as a leader of the Katipunan was difficult. Andres and Oriang had to move from one address to another to avoid the danger of being caught and questioned by colonial authorities. From 1894, they moved several times to different addresses like in Calle Anyahan, to Dulumbayan in Santa Cruz, and in Calle Cervantes in Bambang north of Manila.

On Maundy Thursday of 1896, while Andres was away in Cavite, tragedy struck as fire broke out in their house in Calle Cervantes. Andres and Oriang's possessions were lost in the fire. After the fire, they stayed in the house of Dr. Pio Valenzuela in Binondo. Not long after, Andres and Oriang's baby boy, Andres Jr., who was afflicted with measles, died.

Despite the personal tragedies, Andres continued to work and lead in preparing for a revolution. He knew that when the revolution came and the Katipunan had established a revolutionary government, recognition from other countries was needed.

Andres also tried to secure weapons and aid from Japan with the help of exiled Filipinos in Hong Kong where many nationalist Filipinos who were members of the Propaganda were in self-exile to escape persecution by Spanish authorities. Andres had been in correspondence with them. He tasked Doroteo Cortes to work with exiled Filipinos and arrange the buying of weapons and, upon the start of the revolution, the recognition of independence from Japan.

On May 4, 1896, the Japanese warship Kongo arrived in Manila Bay. Pio Valenzuela organized a meeting with the commander of the visiting Japanese warship, Captain Kanimura. Valenzuela's Japanese friend Jose Moritaro Tagawa arranged the meeting and acted as translator. They met in secret in a Japanese bazar in Plaza Moraga in Binondo. Andres gave a letter addressed to Japanese Emperor Meiji asking for support in their fight for independence. They also gave gifts to the captain: a wooden sculpture and a basket of ripe mangoes to show their hospitality.

Light of Liberty

The Katipunan used a symbol placed on top of its official documents. It was a hand-drawn symbol in baybayin, an old Tagalog script, for the syllable "ka," which stood for *kalayaan* or liberty, and was surrounded by a sunburst of lines. This symbol was the Light of Liberty.

This reflected the ideals of the Katipunan that, once true liberty was acquired, there would be no more suffering in the darkness of cruelty as liberty shone light upon the motherland and its people.

Andres also sought the support and leadership of the exiled Jose Rizal. It would be a dangerous mission to go and talk to Jose as he was closely watched by authorities and the Katipunan's secret was at risk. The task fell to Dr. Pio Valenzuela. To avoid suspicion, he went to Dapitan and pretended to seek medical advice for a blind man because Jose Rizal was also an eye specialist.

Pio arrived in Dapitan on June 21, 1896. He was able to talk to Jose on the evening of July 1. Upon learning about the plans of the Katipunan to start a revolution, Jose refused to join. Instead, Jose offered advice for them to get the support of the rich Filipinos, have the backing of another independent country, and to get enough weapons. Jose told Pio not to think of him but rather to focus on the country in which their countrymen were suffering. Jose was already content in doing his part by helping the people of Dapitan with the projects that he was leading there with the community.

Pio then returned and informed Andres and the rest of the council of Jose's reply. Andres listened and followed Jose's advice. He ordered the procurement of thousands of bolos and planned to establish a company whose earnings would be used to buy weapons from Japan.

Spanish colonial authorities, through their spies, were noticing an increase in meetings with anti-Spanish sentiment. Yet, they were not aware of the existence of the Katipunan itself. They continued to spy and observe that there were activities of recruiting members and gathering of weapons, but they did not know who were the ones behind these activities. With the publication of Kalayaan and the dedication of its members, the Katipunan had around 30,000 members by August of 1896. Andres and the growing Katipunan continued to prepare for a revolution. The Katipunan as a secret organization was then too big of a secret to keep.

The Revolution Begins

In August of 1896, Teodoro Patiño, a katipunero working in the *Diario de Manila*, got into a quarrel with his coworkers who were fellow katipuneros. He went to visit his sister, who was living in a convent, and disclosed information about the Katipunan to her. The latter, along with the convent's mother superior, convinced him to tell everything to Fr. Mariano Gil of Tondo. Patiño then admitted to the Spanish friar about the Katipunan and that supplies from the publishing house were taken by katipuneros working in the printer to print the *Kalayaan*.

Immediately on August 19, 1896, members of

the guardia civil stormed the office and printing press of *Diario de Manila*. Colonial authorities gathered documents and seals of the Katipunan confirming their fears of a planned rebellion of Filipinos against the Spanish colonial government. News spread that the colonial government threatened to declare *Juez de Cuchillo*, or to put to death anyone believed to be part of the conspiracy. Manila was covered in fear following the arrest of many people, both actual members of the Katipunan and those merely suspected of being members of the secret organization.

Upon learning of the Spaniard's discovery of the Katipunan, Andres, his wife and his siblings started packing the important documents of the Katipunan.

They needed to leave Manila at once to avoid being caught. Andres sent out messages to all the chapter leaders of the Katipunan to meet in Balintawak where they would plan their next move. All other members of the Katipunan gathered and hid important documents.

Why the Katipuneros are Depicted as Wearing Red and White

The scheduled meeting with katipuneros fell on the eve of the feast day of San Bartolome or St. Bartholomew the Apostle, the patron saint of Balintawak. St. Bartholomew was depicted as wearing red robes and carrying a blade as he was a martyr and was the patron saint of butchers and bookbinders.

The devotees of St. Bartholomew wore white shirts, red pants, and carried a bolo, a handheld blade used in households and farming. Many of the katipuneros came in the guise of participating in the festivities of the feast. Many of them wore a similar attire to those of the devotees when they went to the assembly called by Andres so as not to draw suspicion from the authorities. It was also a convenient excuse to carry around bolos they could use as weapons.

Andres and the Supreme Council of the Katipunan called for a general assembly in Balintawak on August 23. Some of the katipuneros who went there dressed as women to avoid detection by authorities. More than 2,000 katipuneros arrived in the area. In Kangkong, a barrio in Balintawak, at the house of a Katipunan member, Apolonio Samson, Andres met with the members of the Supreme Council and the leaders of the different chapters in a series of meetings.

Since the Katipunan had been discovered by the Spanish colonial government, they needed to decide if they would start the revolution. They discussed the situation, and most were in favor of starting the uprising by the end of the month.

Andres then went out of the meeting place and addressed the katipuneros gathered around him. He informed them of the decision and asked them if they were ready to fight. The katipuneros shouted their affirmation and raised their fists and bolos. According to Espiridiona Bonifacio's account, Andres was teary-eyed as he saw the willingness of the katipuneros to fight the Spaniards despite the dangers involved. They brought out their cedulas and tore them, a gesture signifying that they were breaking away from the rule of Spain.

They then transferred to the place of Melchora Aquino, known as Tandang Sora, in barrio Banlat. The Supreme Council once again met. As Supreme President, Andres sent out orders and assigned the ranks, responsibilities and areas of command of the chapter leaders. Overnight, the Katipunan became a revolutionary government.

The Cry of Balintawak

Historians have found varying accounts on the location and date of the "cry" or call to fight led by Andres. The locations where the Supreme Council met and where Andres rallied the katipuneros including the tearing of the cedulas in Caloocan are not clear. Sources either say that they happened in Apolonio Samson's place in barrio Kangkong, Melchora Aquino's place near Pasong Tamo in Barrio Banlat, or Juan Ramos's place in Bahay Toro

some time between August 23 and 26 of 1896. The exact location of "Pugad Lawin" is also unclear. The confusion stems from the fact that on those dates, Andres and other Katipunan officials transferred from one place to another and that all of these places were in Balintawak, which at that time was part of Caloocan.

Despite the debate, what was certain was that the katipuneros encamped in these areas decided to finally overthrow Spanish Rule and organized themselves to transform from a secret organization to a revolutionary government, a new government of Filipinos challenging the colonial government ruled by Spaniards.

Andres and the katipuneros prepared for battle. They planned to attack and capture Manila from the provinces of Bulacan in the north, Morong in the east, and Cavite in the south. These planned attacks would occur on the 29th and 30th of August.

On the evening of August 29, Andres led the attack in Mandaluyong. Their forces successfully captured the town hall and they planned to capture the armory of the Spaniards in El Polvorin in San Juan del Monte (now found in the City of San Juan). In the morning of the next day, they encountered a strong Spanish force from El Deposito, the water reservoir, which led to a devastating defeat for the Katipunan. This was known as the Battle of Pinaglabanan.

The fighting in many areas shocked the Spanish population and colonial government in Manila. On the evening of August 30, Spanish Governor General Ramon Blanco declared Martial Law in eight provinces suspected of being heavily organized by the Katipunan namely Manila, Bulacan, Pampanga, Nueva Ecija, Tarlac, Laguna, Cavite, and Batangas. Eventually, these provinces were symbolized by the eight rays of the sun in the Philippine national flag.

The Spanish forces were brutal in seeking revenge against the rebelling Filipinos. Towns that supported katipuneros were burned and scores of townsfolk were all killed. One such town was Nasugbu, Batangas whose inhabitants were killed on a Sunday when many were in church. The katipuneros who tried to defend the town were killed in the battle as well.

Those who were suspected of supporting the Katipunan, young or old, rich or poor, were arrested, tortured and eventually executed. Many also surrendered out of fear. A few ones were exiled far away including Dr. Pio Valenzuela who was imprisoned in Spain for two years.

Despite the problems the revolution faced, many still joined the Katipunan. Other provinces like Tarlac, Bulacan, Batangas and Nueva Ecija, rose up in revolt as well. Many Filipino soldiers serving under the Spanish army deserted and joined the Katipunan. The revolution that Andres started continued to grow as many decided to fight and hope to be finally free from Spanish rule.

In November 1896, Andres and Oriang were reunited. Oriang decided to join her husband in the mountains. She worked with Andres in the responsibilities required in leading the revolution.

Andres and the *katipuneros* retreated to their strongholds in the mountains and waged continuous guerilla warfare against colonial forces. Eventually, Andres established his headquarters in barrio Pantayanin near Pasig. He instructed the different chapters to lead their forces in their respective areas against the Spaniards. Andres was issuing orders as President of *Haring Bayang Katagalugan*.

Haring Bayang Katagalugan

The term "*Haring Bayang Katagalugan*," which could be translated as "Sovereign Tagalog People," was the title of the government Andres headed as the Katipunan waged war against the Spaniards. The use of the word "Tagalog" in the title meant the unified label of everyone in the Philippines referring to the Filipinos as "river people." This title was used in the official documents Andres signed as its president with his signature and official seal.

Unlike Spain which was ruled by a monarch, the Katipunan government was ruled by the People, or was democratic in spirit. This meant that it was intended to be a republic in the making as the revolutionary government waged war against the Spaniards. Despite having no recognition from other independent countries, the Katipunan manned the *Haring Bayan* government and army with Andres as its president.

According to the documents of the Katipunan, in the places they liberated from Spanish control, they conducted elections, assigned ranks and leadership, solicited funds to sustain their campaign, organized attacks, managed the civilian populace, and even officiated marriage rites. This government even had its own anthem called "*Marangal na Dalit ng Katagalugan*" (Honorable Hymn of the Tagalogs) which was composed by musician Julio Nakpil, Andres's close friend.

On November 3, 1896, Jose Rizal was brought back to Manila and was imprisoned in Fort Santiago to undergo trial for his alleged involvement in the Katipunan. Unknown to him, Jose was very important to the Katipunan. Andres wanted to rescue Jose but the latter was closely guarded by Spanish forces. This gave Andres little to no chance of success at a planned rescue leaving Jose to his fate.

A few days after Jose's death, Andres was shown a piece of paper from Jose's sister Trinidad and beloved Josephine Bracken. It contained an untitled poem which Jose wrote. Andres translated this poem to Tagalog so that every Filipino might hear Jose's last offering to the nation. This poem would later on be popularly known as "*Mi Ultimo Adios.*" Andres gave the first title "*Pahimakas*" or final farewell.

Pahimakas

Andres was the first one to translate Jose Rizal's untitled last poem. He did so from Spanish to Tagalog. Andres's translation of the poem was entitled "Pahimakas" or final farewell. Jose's final poem is his farewell to his loved ones and to the motherland with the hope of her salvation. From Jose's 14-stanza poem in Spanish, Andres translated it to 28 stanzas in Tagalog with all lines measuring 12 syllables.

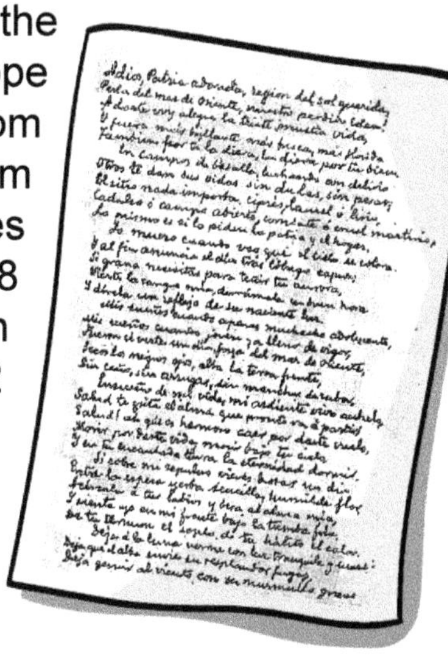

Jose's poem mentioned about sacrificing one's life for the betterment of the motherland which the katipuneros were doing in battle. Despite Jose's refusal to join the Katipunan, he honored the katipuneros in the poem for offering their lives to the motherland. He depicted the sacrifice of those fighting and offering their lives as necessary for the good of the country.

In the poem, Jose wrote:

"In the battlefields, fighting deliriously,
Others offer their lives without doubts
and regret.
It matters not where one falls:
where there is a cypress, laurel or lily;
in the gallows or an open field;
in combat or cruel martyrdom,
all are the same and true if they answer
the call of the motherland."

Conflict in Cavite

Since November of 1896, two of the chapters of the Katipunan in Cavite, Magdalo and Magdiwang, had disagreed over jurisdiction of territories liberated from Spaniards following several victories. Magdiwang was led by Mariano Alvarez while Magdalo was headed by Emilio Aguinaldo's cousin, Baldomero Aguinaldo. In an attempt to solve the disagreements, Andres presided over meetings between the two chapters. However, these meetings did not lead to any resolve.

The Magdalo chapter also refused to recognize Bonifacio's presidency and the validity of the Katipunan government. Another convention was called for on March 22, 1897 in Casa Hacienda in Tejeros, Cavite.

Since the arrival of Andres in Cavite, there had been rumors of him circulating that he was not capable of leading the revolution, that he stole funds from the Katipunan, that he was trying to make himself king of the nation in a misunderstanding of the term "*Haring Bayan*," and that he should not be trusted. Andres only turned a deaf ear to these rumors.

At the convention, Andres found members of both councils questioning the legitimacy of the Katipunan as overall government to head the revolution. They questioned if *Haring Bayang Katagalugan* was truly a democratic government or a monarchy where Andres was the king. But Andres's companions seemed to sense that there was another agenda. It seemed to them that those who were present were pushing for a change of leadership for the entire revolution.

However, Andres was confident that he would win and agreed to the elections on the condition that everyone would respect the outcome of the elections. Andres was nominated as president. The other nominee was Emilio Aguinaldo who was not present at the convention because he needed to lead his troops in a battle.

Emilio Aguinaldo

Emilio Aguinaldo or "Miong," born on March 22, 1869, came from a well-off family. His father served as *gobernadorcillo*. Emilio became a *cabeza de barangay* and eventually the *gobernadorcillo* of Cavite el Viejo (Kawit, Cavite today).

Emilio established the Magdalo chapter of the Katipunan in Cavite where he also led his forces at the start of the Revolution. He became known as a capable leader in battle and was able to lead his forces in two victories in Binakayan and Zapote Bridge where he defeated the Spanish forces.

Andres and Emilio had known each other for some time. Andres personally met Aguinaldo during the latter's initiation into the Katipunan. Andres noted his capacity as a leader when he was able to recruit a lot of members in Cavite. Once, Andres also helped Emilio when the latter had a disagreement with a port official who did not want to give him a license for the boat he used for business.

Andres respected Emilio for being a good leader at a young age and for what he could contribute to the Katipunan and the Revolution. But as the revolution progressed, circumstances changed and the two would come into conflict because of politics in the overall control of the revolution.

There were rumors that the ballots already had names written on them and that there were more ballots than the number of people who attended. After the votes were counted, Emilio Aguinaldo won more votes and was declared the new president. Andres did not protest the outcome. As a sign of respect to Andres, a move was made to have him as vice president, but nobody supported this motion and the elections continued.

Mariano Trias won as Vice-President, followed by General Artemio Ricarte as Captain-General, Emiliano Riego de Dios as Secretary of War. When it was already getting dark, the body decided to shift from secret balloting to public dividing of the house in which case Andres was elected as Secretary of the Interior. From the highest position as Supreme President of the Katipunan, the election made Andres the lowest official in the proposed revolutionary government. He welcomed the results.

After Andres was elected, Daniel Tirona, a member of the Magdalo chapter, stood up and questioned Andres's credentials. He said that the position of Secretary of Interior was too important to be entrusted to someone who was not a lawyer. He mentioned that among them was Jose del Rosario, a lawyer who was well-suited for the post. Tirona appealed to everyone to change their vote from Andres who he said had no educational attainment and instead elect Jose del Rosario.

Andres finally lost his patience at Tirona's insults. Out of anger, he drew his revolver and pointed it towards the direction of Tirona in an act to challenge him in a duel and demanded that the latter take back what he said. Andres was held off by his companions and asked to cool down while Tirona disappeared into the crowd.

Disappointed at the actions and motives of participants of the convention, Andres, as chairman of the convention and President of the *Haring Bayang Katagalugan,* declared all matters approved by the convention null and void. After which, Andres stormed out of the meeting along with his companions.

The next day, Andres and his supporters met on the same location to draft a document to formally nullify the elections of the previous day. The document was known as the *Acta de Tejeros* or the Tejeros Act. It was drafted and signed by Andres and some of those who participated in the Tejeros Convention. The document mentioned the questionable conduct of the elections and reiterated that Andres was still the President of the revolutionary government of the Katipunan.

The events that happened in Tejeros left a heavy feeling in Andres. He wrote to Mariano Alvarez that for his sincerity he received only insults from fellowmen who were not true patriots. He also wrote to Emilio Jacinto mentioning the bad rumors about him in Cavite. Such rumors and many others continued to circulate in Cavite.

Calvary and Death

Andres stayed in Cavite to organize the defense of the liberated towns and to consolidate the actions of revolutionaries. Andres was with his wife Oriang, and his brothers Procopio and Ciriaco, and his men who came from Morong, Bulacan, and Manila. He kept close contact with Katipunan forces under Julio Nakpil, Emilio Jacinto and those in other areas outside Cavite.

Problems arose as Andres and his supporters were met with resistance by Emilio Aguinaldo and his supporters. The latter organized themselves as a revolutionary government not adhering to the declaration of Andres that the outcome of the Tejeros Convention had been voided. This made it more challenging for the katipuneros to face the Spanish forces that were by then retaking the towns of Cavite.

The Cavite leaders believed the rumors that Andres stole money from the Katipunan. Rumors also reached Aguinaldo that Andres threatened to burn down a town if not given supplies. He was also under the impression that Andres was not following the new government formed in Tejeros. Because of this, he ordered the arrest of Andres.

On April 27, 1897, Andres was camped on the outskirts of the town of Limbon when Cavite forces led by Col. Agapito Bonzon arrived. They were welcomed and given food by Andres's men when they suddenly stormed towards the hut where Andres and Oriang were staying. They started shooting the men of Andres.

When Andres went out to investigate the commotion, he was met by Col. Bonzon with armed men who shouted accusations at Andres for stealing money from their movement.

Andres denied the allegations and was trying to diffuse the situation. The man behind him was shot. His brother, Ciriaco, was also shot and killed on the spot.

Andres was trying to stop the commotion when he was shot and hit in the shoulder. One of Col. Bonzon's officers, Ignacio Paua, jumped in and stabbed Andres to the right of his neck. Blood spurted out from his wound, weakening him.

The Title "Supremo"

Andres never called himself as "*Supremo.*" Based on Katipunan documents his official titles were "*Kataas-taasang Pangulo*" (Supreme President), "*Pangulo ng Kataas-taasang Kapulungan*" (President of the Supreme Council) and "President of the *Haring Bayan.*" The title "Supreme President" was used to distinguish the leader of the entire Katipunan from the leader of each Katipunan chapter who was also given the title "President." Some people assumed that the term "*Supremo*" was a sign that Bonifacio wanted to be King. However, "Supremo" was not about supremacy or superiority, it was actually how the educated Spanish-speaking katipuneros refer to him as a translation of his title—*Presidente Supremo.*

Andres, Procopio and their men were taken by Bonzon's men. Andres was carried in a hammock while his brother Procopio was tightly bound.

They were brought to the town of Naic and were locked up in a dark and narrow room, under the stairs of the town's friar house. The thick wooden doors of the stone room were locked and strictly guarded. The Bonifacio brothers were not allowed to have visitors and were prohibited from talking to anyone. They were only fed twice in the three days they were detained. The two were fed with spoiled food and scraps.

On May 1, 1897, Andres and Procopio faced a military tribunal composed of Emilio Aguinaldo's War Council headed by Mariano Noriel and whose members were Tomas Mascardo, Mariano Riego de Dios, Crisostomo Riel, Esteban Ynfante, Sulpicio Antony, and Placido Martinez. It was a trial regarding the accusations hurled at Andres for stealing funds from the Katipunan, and allegedly ordering the assassination of Aguinaldo.

Andres had difficulty in raising his arguments during the trial. He was weak and could barely speak. The wounds he received in the arrest never healed and were already festering. The defense counsel, Placido Martinez, who was also part of the war council did not help either in the well-being of Andres who was severely wounded nor in his defense in trial. Andres was allowed to speak in his defense against the accusations hurled at him, but he was interrupted and was not allowed to continue.

Andres and Procopio were secretly sentenced guilty of treason on May 6, 1897. Emilio Aguinaldo was informed of their decision. The recommendation of the war council was to execute the two.

Oriang saw what happened to her beloved

husband. Throughout this ordeal, Oriang was as close as possible to Andres. Oriang tried to seek an audience with Emilio Aguinaldo to ask that he spare the Bonifacio brothers' lives, but he refused to see her.

Emilio Aguinaldo wanted to reduce the sentence of the Bonifacio brothers to exile in nearby Pico de Loro. But he was urged by the members of the war council, Generals Pio del Pilar and Mariano Noriel, that for the sake of their safety and control of the revolution, the brothers must die. Thus, Emilio Aguinaldo signed a written order and sealed it.

On the morning of May 10, 1897, Major Lazaro Makapagal was given orders to take Andres and Procopio to Mt. Buntis. Major Makapagal had with him a sealed envelope which he was ordered to open only upon reaching Mt. Buntis.

Andres was gravely weak and was carried in a hammock as Procopio, Major Makapagal and his men trekked. They did not reach Mt. Buntis.

Upon reaching the outskirts of Barrio Hulog in Maragondon, Major Makapagal opened the sealed letter and read the order. It was the death sentence to end the life of their two prisoners.

In the middle of the day, in the middle of the jungle, they killed the Father of the Filipino Nation. His vision of *Haring Bayan* died with him. He was killed by his fellow Filipino brothers in arms. Andres's remains were never found.

The Death of Bonifacio

There are different and conflicting accounts on how Andres died.

One account stated that Major Lazaro Makapagal, the one who was ordered to implement the execution of the Bonifacio brothers, wrote historian José P. Santos about the details of the execution. Major Makapagal recounted that, when they opened the letter and found out that it was a death sentence, Andres begged for his life, crying. They shot Procopio first and he died instantly. Andres remained as he was unable to move upon the return of his executioners. As the soldiers were about to shoot the weak Andres, he ran away, and they shot him to death.

However, in an earlier account, Major Makapagal changed his narrative and said that he refused to look when they were killing Andres. Aside from the changing narrative of Major Makapagal, people found it hard to believe that a remarkable man with conviction like Andres would beg for his life that way.

Another account was told to Guillermo Masangkay, a friend of Andres, by two of the supposed executioners of the Bonifacio brothers. They said that they shot Procopio first. They then turned to Andres and hacked him to death with bolos, because they did not want to waste their bullets. It was said that this story became the basis of the famous rhyme, "Andres Bonifacio, atapang-a-tao. Aputol a kamay hindi a-takbo...." or "Andres Bonifacio, a brave man. Arm cut off, he will not run..."

However way Andres died, the tragedy of the Revolution was that he was killed by fellow Filipinos who were a part of the revolution he fathered.

The Legacy of Andres Bonifacio

Andres dreamed of a society that was free and just. Although his death was tragic and the *Haring Bayan* did not materialize, many Filipinos continued the cause of freedom for which Andres lived and fought. The Revolution that Andres started eventually defeated the Spaniards and allowed for the proclamation of Philippine Independence in 1898.

This brought an end to the three centuries rule of Spain. This also led to the creation of the First Philippine Republic in 1899 which was later recognized as the first constitutional democratic republic in Asia.

The people also continued to carry the flag of his memory. Since the end of the Revolution, Andres was already lauded by Filipinos as one of the prime heroes of the Philippines. He was dubbed by historians as "The Father of the Philippine Revolution," "The Father of the Filipino Nation," and "The Father of Philippine Democracy" due to his ideals of nationhood and his leadership at the start of the revolution.

Many of his monuments were erected close to where the common people are—in plazas and places where they work and earn an honest living like in Tutuban and Caloocan.

Even under American rule and until today, Filipinos have openly honored Andres. When people would have grievances against the government, they would hold protests under the gaze of Bonifacio at Liwasang Bonifacio during his birthday.

On February 23, 1918, Act No. 2760 was passed by Filipino lawmakers which allowed the building of a memorial for Andres as well as the creation of a national committee to oversee the project. However, its implementation was delayed by over a decade as American colonial authorities resisted its implementation.

The cornerstone for the Bonifacio monument was finally laid in a ceremony on Andres's 66th birth anniversary in 1929. A competition was held for the design and construction of the monument. Second place went to architect Juan Nakpil, son of Oriang and her second husband Julio Nakpil, with sculptor Ambrosio Garcia. The winning design was of Guillermo Tolentino. The government allocated funds for the project but contributions from the public also poured in to bring Andres's monument to full scale. In 1933, the Andres Bonifacio Monument was erected in Caloocan.

Bonifacio Monument

The monument of Andres Bonifacio was inaugurated in 1933 in Caloocan, the area where Andres started the revolution in 1896. Standing 14 meters in height, it was designed by National Artist Guillermo Tolentino assisted by sculptors Anastacio Caedo and Francesco Riccardo Monti.

The monument is filled with symbolism. The winged figure on top of the 14-meter obelisk symbolizes Filipino victory over Spanish rule. Behind the monument shows the three martyred priests—Fathers Mariano Gomez, Jose Burgos and Jacinto Zamora or the Gomburza.

On the sides are sculptures of Filipinos struggling against the cruelty of colonial rule. At the front of the monument is Andres with Emilio Jacinto and their men.

Andres is standing looking calm and dignified as he holds a bolo and a pistol. National Artist for Sculpture Napoleon Abueva, a student of Guillermo Tolentino, interprets Andres's calm and calculating look as his quiet dignity and confidence amidst the on-going turmoil around him, which echoes the strong and indominable spirit of Filipinos.

In 1921, by virtue of Act No. 2946 enacted by the Philippine Legislature, Andres's day of birth was proclaimed a national public holiday. Bonifacio Day was created to commemorate his heroism. By practice, anonymous Filipino heroes were also commemorated on the same day.

Andres's poem, "*Pag-ibig sa Tinubuang Bayan*," was set to music and sung during the dark days of Martial Law and became a popular protest song against the dictatorship towards the People Power Revolution of 1986.

Filipino scholars continue to write about Andres, the Katipunan, and the Revolution. Some of the notable historians who wrote about Andres include Epifanio de los Santos, Teodoro Agoncillo, Milagros Guerrero and Zeus Salazar.

Later on, more documents of the Katipunan resurfaced. The General Military Archives of Madrid turned over to the National Historical Commission of the Philippines (NHCP) digital copies of more than 150 Katipunan documents that were seized by the Spanish colonial authorities during the time of Andres. These documents were studied by historian Jim Richardson who published the translated and annotated documents in his book *Light of Liberty: Documents and Studies on the Katipunan*, 1892-1897. These provided more insights as to how the Katipunan operated and what Andres was like as a leader.

With new sources and more information, new perspectives on Andres's life and leadership could be observed. This included the *de facto* government he led at the start of the Revolution which had a structured organization and controlled territories in different parts of the Philippines. It governed communities and even had elected officials, a flag and an anthem.

Bonifacio the Philippine President

In 1993, three historians, Milagros Guerrero, Emmanuel Encarnacion, and Ramon Villegas petitioned the Ramos Administration of the Philippines to consider Andres as a president of the Philippines and to give him a State Funeral. According to these three historians, when the Katipunan became a *de facto* government at the start of the Revolution, Andres, as the Katipunan's leader, became the first President of the Filipino Nation. This was their position in their studies and their petition. However, their petition was denied by the then National Historical Institute (now the NHCP).

Currently, Andres is not listed as a Philippine president though some historians continue to petition for him to be recognized as such. These historians argue that the presidents of the Philippines did not serve under a single continuing republic; it had three Republics and one Commonwealth government which was not an independent republic. However, Philippine presidents are counted similarly to the way the presidents of the United States are counted—listing

45 presidents from the start of a single two-century old republic.

Historians who support the petition to recognize Andres as a Philippine president propose listing presidents according to their respective republics, with the inclusion of revolutionary governments. With this perspective, Andres can be listed as a President of the *Haring Bayan* or the government which he led.

In 2013, the 150th birth anniversary of Andres Bonifacio was commemorated and in line with this, the National Historical Commission inaugurated the Museum of the Katipunan in San Juan City.

Several performances in art, film, television and theater were also performed during this time. The life and heroism of Andres is depicted in many films and television shows. The movie "*Andres Bonifacio: Ang Supremo*" released in 1964 is the oldest known movie about Andres.

His character would be present in historical films like "*Jose Rizal*" (1998) and TV show "*Bayani*" (1995). The film "*Supremo*" (2012) directed by Alfred Vargas and "*Bonifacio: Unang Pangulo*" (2014) are films showing an updated view of Andres. The television drama series "*Katipunan*" shown in 2013 by GMA Network showed the struggles of Andres and the Katipunan in preparing and fighting the Revolution. Andres in the recent years has also become the subject of art by young artists as part of the growing trend of looking at our history for inspiration.

People still find the life and works of Andres relevant today. Andres continues to serve as an inspiration for everyone to fight for social justice and freedom for all. His ideals remind us that building a nation means to take care of one another and to work together for the good of the motherland.

Andres Bonifacio, A *Bayani*

A *bayani* or a hero is someone who fights alongside his or her people for a better future for all. A *bayani* also inspires others to act despite the dangers and uncertainties along the way. Andres, as "Maypagasa," truly gave hope as a *bayani*. He is considered a *bayani* and a leader who led the fight for Philippine independence from Spain. We also see him as a *bayani* in the following ways:

1. **Andres taught us to value freedom.**

   For Andres, building a nation was not just the formal establishment of a government but also included upholding the welfare and freedom of its people. Without freedom, everyone suffers under injustice, lies, and fear. Andres and the katipuneros overcame these with courage, hope, and the desire for truth and justice. Like many after them, our heroes fought and died for the freedoms that we enjoy today. Being a *bayani* means loving one's country by protecting the freedom and dignity of its people and looking out for one another.

2. **Andres taught us that our talents and interests can contribute to society.**

   We sacrifice the activities that we love, for it seems that they are not worthwhile and immediately rewarding. Andres believed that no act is wasted if it is pursued as a contribution to one's motherland. Andres found time to pursue his interests in theater, reading books, and writing literature as he pursued the goals of the Katipunan. He showed that art and creativity can help improve society and help in one's advocacy. Being a *bayani* means offering one's talents and skills for the good of others and for the honor of the country.

3. **Andres showed that leading people means empowering them.**

   In leading the Katipunan, he listened to his colleagues, recognized their skills and trusted them to get things done. He recognized the writing skills of Emilio Jacinto and gave way to the publishing of the *Kartilya*. He recognized the desire of Pio to manage the Kalayaan enabling their organization's ideals to spread and their number to grow. As an organizer, Andres kept an open and humble mind which attracted like-minded people and leaders that ultimately strengthened their organization. Being a *bayani* means being a leader that inspires others to become leaders as well.

4. **Andres shared his ideals and inspired many others to act.**

   Andres wrote that there was no greater and purer form of love other than the love of one's country. Andres shared this with everyone. In his writings and speeches, he used a language his countrymen could best relate to and understand. He did not keep his vision of a future of freedom and enlightenment to himself nor to only a few people. In organizing the Katipunan, he invited everyone, whether rich or poor, educated or not, to free the motherland. Andres taught us that being a *bayani* means to share what we believe in so that we may also inspire others to act.

5. **Andres fought fear with hope.**

   Andres hoped to see his fellowmen free from suffering under centuries of colonial rule. This hope that the Philippines could be a free nation triumphed over the fear that the colonizers used for centuries and enabled him to organize the Katipunan even when it was dangerous to do so. This hope sustained the revolution that Andres led despite his untimely demise. Hope was what carried the revolution to victory, and which continues to burn in our quest for a better society. Like Andres, a.k.a. *Maypagasa*, being a *bayani* means spreading a message of hope, even in the darkest of times, which can light the way towards a better future.

Let us remember Andres as a *bayani*. Andres who did not only teach us courage, but who also taught us to love one another. That is how he imagined us building the nation.

Bibliography

Agoncillo, Teodoro A. *The Revolt of the Masses: The Story of Bonifacio and the Katipunan*. Quezon City, University of the Philippines Press, 1956.

Agoncillo, Teodoro A. and Silvino V. Epistola, trans. *The Writings and Trial of Andres Bonifacio*. Manila: Antonio J. Villegas; Manila Bonifacio Centennial Commission; University of the Philippines, 1963.

Almario, Virgilio S. *Panitikan ng Rebolusyon(g 1896): Isang Paglingon at Katipunan ng mga Akda nina Bonifacio at Jacinto*. Manila: Komisyon sa Wikang Filipino, 2013.

Alvarez, Santiago V. *The Katipunan and the Revolution: Memoirs of a General*, edited and translated by Paula Carolina S. Malay. Quezon City: Ateneo de Manila University Press, 1992.

Alzona, Encarnacion. J*ulio Nakpil and the Philippine Revolution*. Manila: Carmelo and Bauermann, Inc., 1964.

Cahiles, Weng D. *What Kids Should Know About Andres and the Katipunan*. Quezon City: Adarna House, 2013.

Canseco, Telesforo. *Kasaysayan ng Paghihimagsik ng mga Pilipino sa Cavite, 1897 (salin ni José Rhommel B. Hernandez)*. Quezon City: Philippine Dominican Center for Institutional Studies, 1999.

Capino, Diosdado G. *Stories of Andres Bonifacio: His Life, Character and Teachings*. Quezon City: Manlapaz Publishing Company, 1967.

Chua, Michael Charleston "Xiao". *The Case for Andres Bonifacio as the First President of the Philippines (An excerpt)*. Esquire, March 2015: 74-76.

Cristobal, Adrian E. *The Tragedy of the Revolution*. Makati: Studio 5 Publishing, 1997.

Guerrero, Milagros C. and Michael Charleston "Xiao" B. Chua. Bonifacio: *Ang Unang Pangulo: Backstories to the Movie for Teachers and Students*. Mandaluyong City: Anvil Publishing, Inc., 2014.

Guerrero, Milagros C., Emmanuel N. Encarnacion and Ramon N. Villegas. *Andres Bonifacio and the 1896 Revolution*, Sulyap Kultura, Second Quarter 1996: 3-12.

Ileto, Reynaldo C., *Filipinos and Their Revolution: Event, Discourse, and Historiography*. Hawaii: University of Hawaii Press, 1998.

Llanes, Ferdinand C., ed. *Katipunan: Isang Pambansang Kilusan*. Quezon City: Trinitas Publishing, Inc., 1994.

Maceda, Teresita Gimenez. *The Katipunan Discourse on Kaginhawaan:*

Vision and Configuration of a Just and Free Society, Kasarinlan: A Philippine Quarterly of Third World Studies, Vol. 14, Num. 2 (1998): 77-94.

Manuel, Espiridion Arsenio. *New Data on Andres Bonifacio: Manila's Foremost Hero*. Typescript, 1989.

Medina, Isagani R., ed. Ilang *Talata Tungkol sa Paghihimagsik (Revolucion) Nang 1896-1897* Isinulat ni Carlos Ronquillo y Valdez (Hongkong 1898). Quezon City: University of the Philippines Press, 1996.

Navarro, Arthur M. and Raymund Arthur G. Abejo, eds. *Wika, Panitikan, Sining at Himagsikan*. Quezon City: LIKAS, 1998.

Nunag, Angelito, S. *Mga Bagong Pagtingin kay Andres Bonifacio at sa Katipunan*. Saliksik E-Journal 3, Num. 2 (2014): 92-141.

Ocampo, Ambeth R. *Bones of Contention: The Bonifacio Lectures*. Pasig City: Anvil Publishing, Inc., 2001.

Ricarte, Artemio. *Himagsikan Nang Manga Pilipino Laban sa Kastila*. Yokohama, Hapon: Artemio Ricarte, 1927.

Richardson, Jim. *Light of Liberty: Documents and Studies on the Katipunan, 1892-1897*. Quezon City: ADMU Press, 2013.

Salazar, Zeus A. Agosto 29-30, 1896: *Ang Pagsalakay ni Bonifacio sa Maynila* (salin ni Monico M. Atienza). Quezon City: Miranda Bookstore, 1995.

Salazar, Zeus A. *Si Andres Bonifacio at ang Kabayanihang Pilipino, Bagong Kasaysayan: Mga Pag-aaral sa Kasaysayan ng Pilipinas Lathalain Blg. 2*. Mandaluyong City: Palimbagang Kalawakan, 1997.

Santos, José P. *Si Andres Bonifacio at ang Himagsikan, Ikalawang Pagkalimbag*. Gerona, Tarlac: José Paez Santos, 1935.

Ventura, Sylvia Mendez. *Supremo: The Story of Andres Bonifacio*. Makati City: Tahanan Books for Young Readers, 2001.

Yson, Reymar Tecson. *The Cry of Balintawak: Critical Analysis* (unpublished Masters Thesis). Manila: MLQU, 2016

Websites

Katipunan Documents and Studies: http://www.kasaysayan-kkk.info
Presidential Museum and Library: http://malacanang.gov.ph

Acknowledgment

We are forever grateful for mentors who made us know Bonifacio a little better: Milagros C. Guerrero, Zeus A. Salazar, Jaime B. Veneracion, Ambeth R. Ocampo, and Jim Richardson. We would like to thank Wowie and Regine for this opportunity to bring the story of Andres closer to children.

Xiao: I would like to thank the National Historical Commission of the Philippines for the opportunity to write the official state documentary with Red Root Artists Cooperative entitled "Maypagasa: Ang Bantayog ni Andres Bonifacio." The updated information and insights collected for the said production are reflected in this humble work. And to my parents Charles and Vilma for teaching Michelle, Mark and me to be better citizens of the Nation, thank you. I dedicate this to Sir Rene Villanueva, who told me that historians should write for children days before he died. With this book, we have fulfilled his wish.

John Ray: Special thanks to my friends Cesar, Keith, Paula and Felice for keeping me company while writing this book. Many thanks to my sister Diana for continuing to send me cute dog memes. Thank you, too, to my Tita Brenda and to my parents Maximo and Yolanda for continuing to support my humble career and passion in history and for teaching me always to seek wisdom, righteousness, and compassion in my every action.

About the Author

Michael Charleston "Xiao" Chua is an assistant professorial lecturer at the De La Salle University History Department and a senior lecturer at the UP Department of Broadcast Communication. He finished his Bachelor's and Master's degree in History and is a Ph.D. Anthropology candidate at the University of the Philippines. He served as Vice President and currently Public Relations Officer of the Philippine Historical Association. He is the co-author of "Bonifacio: Ang Unang Pangulo" and was historical consultant of the television shows "History with Lourd," "Katipunan" and "Ilustrado." He created the "Xiao Time" television segment for the government television channel episodes of which are still accessible online. He currently writes a Saturday English column at the Manila Times and a Filipino Sunday column in Abante. He is the most active historian in the Philippine media.

John Ray Ramos is a part-time intructor at the Ateneo de Manila University History Department and at the Institute of Formation and Religous Studies. He finished his bachelor's degree in History and is taking his Master's degree in Public Administration at the University of the Philippines. He is pursuing a multidisciplinary career in the field of public history, heritage conservation and cultural policy. He co-founded PROYEKTO, a project-based movement aimed at promoting history and heritage awareness and education. He served as the Chapter Commander of the Sucesos Chapter of the Order of the Knights of Rizal. He is the author of "Bayani Biographies: Jose Rizal" also published by Kahel Press.

www.ingramcontent.com/pod-product-compliance
Ingram Content Group UK Ltd.
Pitfield, Milton Keynes, MK11 3LW, UK
UKHW021651190726
13853UKWH00001B/198